From this day forward I will earn, save, and play for a brighter tomorrow and a pleasant today.

A land of plenty where money was treasured and used
with every care and measure.

After his dream, he awoke with a smile on his face. Spencer told his family that he dreamed of a faraway place.

I can use it for charity, clothes, or a toy.

Thirty cents left, that is mine to enjoy.

Spencer looked at his change
with calm intuition.
"I will save twenty cents for
my college tuition."

"Surely," said Spencer, "now I can spend.
Fifty cents left what should I do then?"

"Seventy cents left, what should I do? Surely," said Spencer, "now I can spend." His uncle said, "Remember what comes next young man, put twenty cents away for your investment plan."

"Ninety cents left, what should I do? Surely," said Spencer, "now I can spend." His mother said, "Remember what comes next my son. Two dimes must go in your Rainy Day Fund."

He remembered his
grandfather's words,
"What comes first my son?
A dime goes to God for all
He has done."

But his father said, "What should you do then?"

His brother, Jordan, said, "Here's a dollar for you. You worked hard for that dollar now what should you do?" Spencer looked at the dollar wanting to spend.

His dreams took him to
a faraway place where he
saw his loved ones.

Spencer began to dream about all his dollar could do.

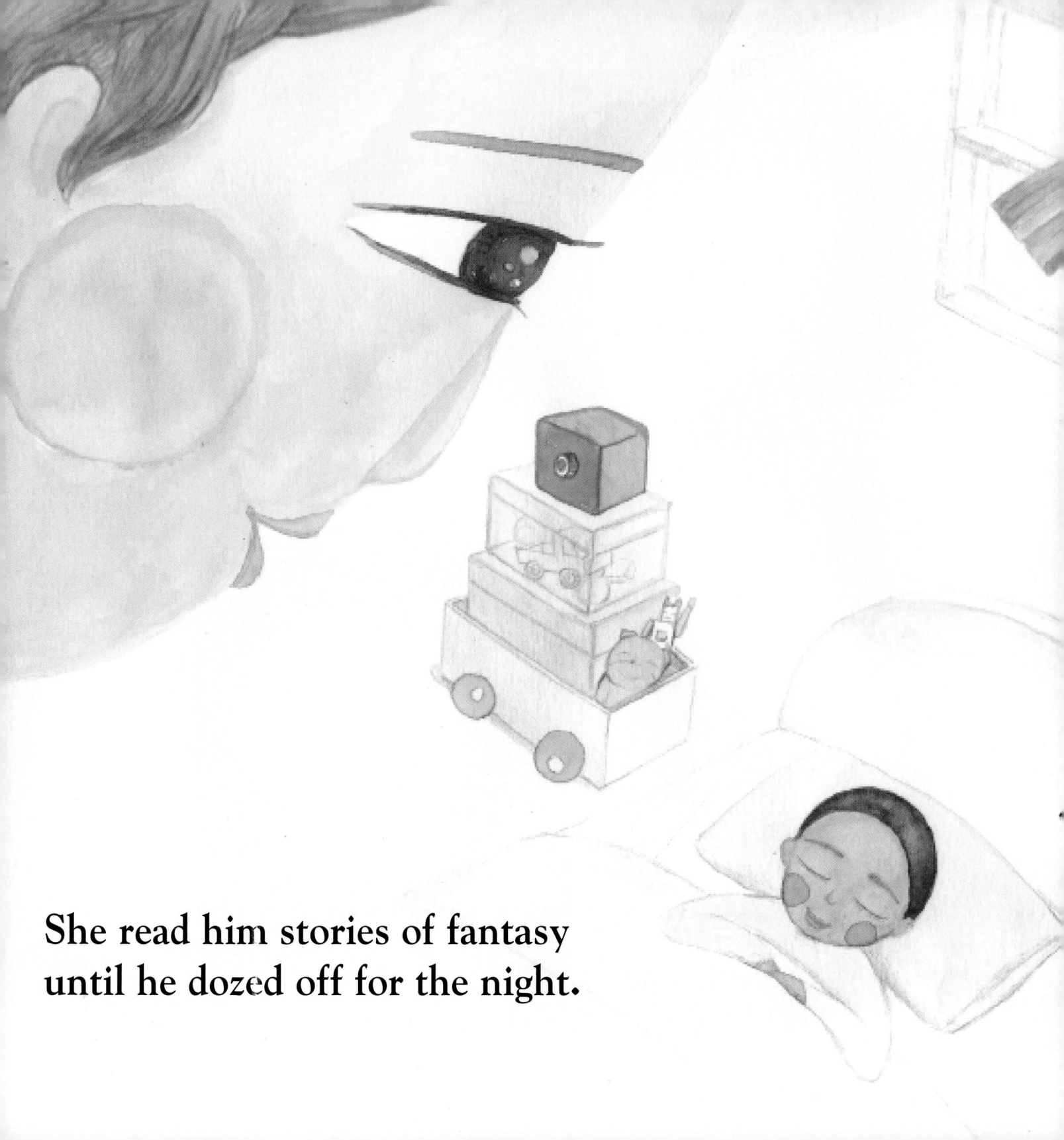

She read him stories of fantasy
until he dozed off for the night.

Every night when it was time for bed, his mother kissed him and tucked him in tight.

He loved money so much, he
even dreamed about money.

He loved to count money.

He loved to
play with money.

He loved to save money.

Spencer loved money.

Once upon a time, there was an
enterprising young boy named Spencer.

Dedication
This book is dedicated to my nephews Aaron, Eric, Jordan, and Spencer.
They are my inspiration and the reason I want to leave a legacy of wealth.